Congressional
Research
Service

The New START Treaty: Central Limits and Key Provisions

Amy F. Woolf
Specialist in Nuclear Weapons Policy

February 14, 2012

Congressional Research Service

7-5700

www.crs.gov

R41219

CRS Report for Congress ————————————————

Summary

The United States and Russia signed the New START Treaty on April 8, 2010. The Senate Foreign Relations Committee and Senate Armed Services Committee both held hearings on the treaty. The U.S. Senate gave its advice and consent to ratification on December 22, 2010, by a vote of 71-26. Both houses of the Russian parliament—the Duma and Federation Council—approved the treaty in late January 2011, and it entered into force on February 5, 2011, after Secretary of State Clinton and Foreign Minister Lavrov exchanged the instruments of ratification.

New START provides the parties with seven years to reduce their forces, and will remain in force for a total of 10 years. It limits each side to no more than 800 deployed and nondeployed ICBM and SLBM launchers and deployed and nondeployed heavy bombers equipped to carry nuclear armaments. Within that total, each side can retain no more than 700 deployed ICBMs, deployed SLBMs, and deployed heavy bombers equipped to carry nuclear armaments. The treaty also limits each side to no more than 1,550 deployed warheads; those are the actual number of warheads on deployed ICBMs and SLBMs, and one warhead for each deployed heavy bomber.

New START contains detailed definitions and counting rules that will help the parties calculate the number of warheads that count under the treaty limits. Moreover, the delivery vehicles and their warheads will count under the treaty limits until they are converted or eliminated according to the provisions described in the treaty's Protocol. These provisions are far less demanding than those in the original START Treaty and will provide the United States and Russia with far more flexibility in determining how to reduce their forces to meet the treaty limits.

The monitoring and verification regime in the New START Treaty is less costly and complex than the regime in START. Like START, though, it contains detailed definitions of items limited by the treaty; provisions governing the use of national technical means (NTM) to gather data on each side's forces and activities; an extensive database that identifies the numbers, types, and locations of items limited by the treaty; provisions requiring notifications about items limited by the treaty; and inspections allowing the parties to confirm information shared during data exchanges.

New START does not limit current or planned U.S. missile defense programs. It does ban the conversion of ICBM and SLBM launchers to launchers for missile defense interceptors, but the United States never intended to pursue such conversions when deploying missile defense interceptors. Under New START, the United States can deploy conventional warheads on its ballistic missiles, but these will count under the treaty limit on nuclear warheads. The United States may deploy a small number of these systems during the time that New START is in force.

The Obama Administration and outside analysts argue that New START will strengthen strategic stability and enhance U.S. national security. They contend that New START will contribute to U.S. nuclear nonproliferation goals by convincing other nations that the United States is serious about its obligations under the NPT. This might convince more nations to cooperate with the United States in pressuring nations who are seeking their own nuclear weapons.

Critics, however, question whether the treaty serves U.S. national security interests, as Russia was likely to reduce its forces with or without an arms control agreement and because the United States and Russia no longer need arms control treaties to manage their relationship. Some also consider the U.S.-Russian arms control process to be a distraction from the more important issues on the nonproliferation agenda.

Contents

Tables

Contacts

Introduction

The United States and Russia signed a new strategic arms reduction treaty—known as New START—on April 8, 2010.[1] This treaty is designed to replace the 1991 Strategic Arms Reductions Treaty (START), which expired, after 15 years of implementation, on December 5, 2009.[2] The U.S. Senate provided its advice and consent to ratification of New START on December 22, 2010, by a vote of 71-26. The Russian parliament, with both the Duma and Federation Council voting, did so on January 25 and January 26, 2011. The treaty entered into force on February 5, 2011, after Secretary of State Clinton and Foreign Minister Lavrov exchanged the instruments of ratification. New START supersedes the 2002 Strategic Offensive Reductions Treaty (known as the Moscow Treaty), which has now lapsed.[3] New START provides the parties with seven years to reduce their forces, and it will remain in force for a total of 10 years.

Presidents Obama and Medvedev outlined their goals for the negotiations on a new START Treaty in early April 2009. In a joint statement issued after they met in London, they indicated that the subject of the new agreement "will be the reduction and limitation of strategic offensive arms."[4] This statement indicated that the new treaty would not address missile defenses, nonstrategic nuclear weapons, or nondeployed stockpiles of nuclear weapons. The Presidents also agreed that they would seek to reduce their forces to levels below those in the 2002 Moscow Treaty, and that the new agreement would "mutually enhance the security of the Parties and predictability and stability in strategic offensive forces, and will include effective verification measures drawn from the experience of the Parties in implementing the START Treaty."

The Presidents further refined their goals for New START, and gave the first indications of the range they were considering for the limits in the treaty, in a Joint Understanding signed at their summit meeting in Moscow in July 2009. They agreed that the new treaty would restrict each party to between 500 and 1,100 strategic delivery vehicles and between 1,500 and 1,675 associated warheads. They also agreed that the new treaty would contain "provisions on definitions, data exchanges, notifications, eliminations, inspections and verification procedures, as well as confidence building and transparency measures, as adapted, simplified, and made less costly, as appropriate, in comparison to the START Treaty."[5]

The New START Treaty follows many of the same conventions as the 1991 START Treaty. It contains detailed definitions and counting rules that the parties will use to identify the forces limited by the treaty. It also mandates that the parties maintain an extensive database that will

---

[1] The treaty is officially titled the Treaty Between the United States of America and the Russian Federation on Measures for the Further Reduction and Limitation of Strategic Offensive Arms. The text of the Treaty, its Protocol, annexes, and article-by-article analysis can be found at http://www.state.gov/t/avc/newstart/c44126 htm.

[2] For a brief summary of the original START Treaty, as well as a review of the U.S.-Russian negotiations on the new START Treaty see CRS Report R40084, *Strategic Arms Control After START: Issues and Options*, by Amy F. Woolf.

[3] The Moscow Treaty was to remain in force until December 31, 2012, unless replaced by a subsequent treaty. For details on this agreement see CRS Report RL31448, *Nuclear Arms Control: The Strategic Offensive Reductions Treaty*, by Amy F. Woolf.

[4] The White House, Office of the Press Secretary, *Joint Statement by President Dmitriy Medvedev of the Russian Federation and President Barack Obama of the United States of America*, April 1, 2009. http://www.whitehouse.gov/the_press_office/Joint-Statement-by-President-Dmitriy-Medvedev-of-the-Russian-Federation-and-President-Barack-Obama-of-the-United-States-of-America/.

[5] The White House, Office of the Press Secretary, Joint Understanding by Obama, Medvedev on Weapon Negotiations. July 8, 2009. http://www.america.gov/st/texttrans-english/2009/July/20090708154724xjsnommis0.7355005 html.

---

describe the locations, numbers, and technical characteristics of weapons limited by the treaty. It allows the parties to use several types of exhibitions and on-site inspections to confirm information in the database and to monitor forces and activities limited by the treaty.

But the new treaty is not simply an extension of START. The United States and Soviet Union negotiated the original START Treaty during the 1980s, during the latter years of the Cold War, when the two nations were still adversaries and each was still wary of the capabilities and intentions of the other. Many of the provisions in the original treaty reflect the uncertainty and suspicion that were evident at that time. The New START Treaty is a product of a different era and a different relationship between the United States and Russia.[6] In some ways, its goals remain the same—the parties have still sought provisions that would allow for predictability and transparency in their current forces and future intentions. But, the United States and Russia have streamlined and simplified the central limits and the monitoring and verification provisions. The new treaty does not contain layers of limits and sublimits; each side can determine its own mix of land-based intercontinental ballistic missiles (ICBMs), submarine-launched ballistic missiles (SLBMs) and heavy bombers. Moreover, in the current environment, the parties were far less concerned with choking off avenues for potential evasion schemes than they were with fostering continued cooperation and openness between the two sides.

Central Limits and Key Provisions

Central Limits

Limits on Delivery Vehicles

The New START Treaty contains three central limits on U.S. and Russian strategic offensive nuclear forces; these are displayed in **Table 1**, below. First, it limits each side to no more than 800 deployed and nondeployed ICBM and SLBM launchers and deployed and nondeployed heavy bombers equipped to carry nuclear armaments. Second, within that total, it limits each side to no more than 700 deployed ICBMs, deployed SLBMs, and deployed heavy bombers equipped to carry nuclear armaments. Third, the treaty limits each side to no more than 1,550 deployed warheads. Deployed warheads include the actual number of warheads carried by deployed ICBMs and SLBMs, and one warhead for each deployed heavy bomber equipped for nuclear armaments. **Table 1** compares these limits to those in the 1991 START Treaty and the 2002 Moscow Treaty.

According to New START's Protocol[7] a deployed ICBM launcher is "an ICBM launcher that contains an ICBM and is not an ICBM test launcher, an ICBM training launcher, or an ICBM launcher located at a space launch facility." A deployed SLBM launcher is a launcher installed on an operational submarine that contains an SLBM and is not intended for testing or training. A deployed mobile launcher of ICBMs is one that contains an ICBM and is not a mobile test

---

[6] U.S. Department of State, Bureau of Verification, Compliance and Implementation, *Comparison of START Treaty, Moscow Treaty, and New START Treaty*, Fact Sheet, Washington, DC, April 8, 2010, http://www.state.gov/t/vci/rls/ 139901 htm.

[7] New START is a three-part document. It includes the Treaty, a Protocol, and technical annexes. All three parts will be submitted to the Senate for advice and consent.

launcher or a mobile launcher of ICBMs located at a space launch facility. These deployed launchers can be based only at ICBM bases. A deployed ICBM or SLBM is one that is contained in a deployed launcher. Nondeployed launchers are, therefore, those that are used for testing or training, those that are located at space launch facilities, or those that are located at deployment areas or on submarines but do not contain a deployed ICBM or SLBM.

Table 1. Limits in START, Moscow Treaty, and New START

Treaty	START (1991)	Moscow Treaty (2002)	New START (2010)
Limits on Delivery Vehicles	1,600 strategic nuclear delivery vehicles	No limits	800 deployed and nondeployed ICBM launchers, SLBM launchers and heavy bombers equipped to carry nuclear weapons Within the 800 limit, 700 deployed ICBMs, SLBMs, and heavy bombers equipped to carry nuclear weapons
Limits on Warheads	6,000 warheads attributed to ICBMs, SLBMs, and heavy bombers 4,900 warheads attributed to ICBMs and SLBMs 1,100 warheads attributed to mobile ICBMs 1,540 warheads attributed to heavy ICBMs	1,700-2,200 deployed strategic warheads No sublimits	1,550 deployed warheads No sublimits
Limits on Throwweight	3,600 metric tons	No limit	No limit

Source: State Department fact sheets.

The New START Treaty does not limit the number of nondeployed ICBMs or nondeployed SLBMs. It does, however, state that these missiles must be located at facilities that are known to be within the infrastructure that supports and maintains ICBMs and SLBMs. These include "submarine bases, ICBM or SLBM loading facilities, maintenance facilities, repair facilities for ICBMs or SLBMs, storage facilities for ICBMs or SLBMs, conversion or elimination facilities for ICBMs or SLBMs, test ranges, space launch facilities, and production facilities." Nondeployed ICBMs and SLBMs may also be in transit between these facilities, although Article IV of the treaty indicates that this time in transit should be "no more than 30 days."

The parties will share information on the locations of these missiles in the database they maintain under the treaty and notify each other when they move these systems. These provisions are designed to allow each side to keep track of the numbers and locations of nondeployed missiles and to deter efforts to stockpile hidden, uncounted missiles. A party would be in violation of the treaty if one of its nondeployed missiles were spotted at a facility not included on the list, or if one were found at a location different from the one listed for that missile in the database.[8]

According to the Protocol to New START, a deployed heavy bomber is one that is equipped for nuclear armaments but is not a "test heavy bomber or a heavy bomber located at a repair facility or at a production facility." Moreover, a heavy bomber is equipped for nuclear armaments if it is "equipped for long-range nuclear ALCMs, nuclear air-to-surface missiles, or nuclear bombs." All deployed heavy bombers must be located at air bases, which are defined as facilities "at which deployed heavy bombers are based and their operation is supported." If an air base cannot support the operations of heavy bombers, then the treaty does not consider it to be available for the basing of heavy bombers, even though they may land at such bases under some circumstances. Test heavy bombers can be based only at heavy bomber flight test centers and non-deployed heavy bombers other than test heavy bombers can be located only at repair facilities or production facilities for heavy bombers. Each party may have no more than 10 test heavy bombers.

Heavy bombers that are not equipped for long range nuclear ALCMs, nuclear air-to-surface missiles, or nuclear bombs will not count under the treaty limits. However, the treaty does specify that, "within the same type, a heavy bomber equipped for nuclear armaments shall be distinguishable from a heavy bomber equipped for non-nuclear armaments." Moreover, if a party does convert some bombers within a given type so that they are no longer equipped to carry nuclear weapons, it cannot base the nuclear and non-nuclear bombers at the same air base, unless otherwise agreed by the parties.

Hence, the United States could reduce the number of bombers that count under the treaty limits by altering some of its B-52 bombers so that they no longer carry nuclear weapons and by basing them at a separate base from those that still carry nuclear weapons. In addition, if the United States converted all of the bombers of a given type, so that none of them could carry nuclear armaments, then none of the bombers of that type would count under the New START treaty. This provision would allow the United States to remove its B-1 bombers from treaty accountability. They no longer carry nuclear weapons, but they still counted under the old START Treaty and have never been altered so that they could not carry nuclear weapons. The conversion rules that would affect the B-1 bombers are described below.

Limits on Warheads

Table 1 summarizes the warheads limits in START, the Moscow Treaty, and the New START Treaty. Two factors stand out in this comparison. First, the original START Treaty contained several sublimits on warheads attributed to different types of strategic weapons, in part because the United States wanted the treaty to impose specific limits on elements of the Soviet force that were deemed to be "destabilizing." Therefore, START sought to limit the Soviet force of heavy ICBMs by cutting in half the number of warheads deployed on these missiles, and to limit future Soviet deployments of mobile ICBMs. The Moscow Treaty and New START, in contrast, contain only a single limit on the aggregate number of deployed warheads. They provide each nation with the freedom to mix their forces as they see fit. This change reflects, in part, a lesser concern with Cold War models of strategic and crisis stability. It also derives from the U.S. desire to maintain flexibility in determining the structure of its own nuclear forces.

---

[8] Each individual missile will be identified in the database by a "unique identifier," which will, in most cases, be the serial number affixed to the missile during production.

Table 1 also highlights how the planned numbers of warheads in the U.S. and Russian strategic forces have declined in the years since the end of the Cold War. Before START entered into force in 1991, each side had more than 10,000 warheads on its strategic offensive delivery vehicles. If the parties implement the New START Treaty, that number will have declined by more than 80%. However, although all three treaties limit warheads, each uses different definitions and counting rules to determine how many warheads each side has deployed on its strategic forces.

Under START, the United States and Russia did not actually count deployed warheads. Instead, each party counted the launchers—ICBM silos, SLBM launch tubes, and heavy bombers—deployed by the other side. Under the terms of the treaty, they then assumed that each operational launcher contained an operational missile, and each operational missile carried an "attributed" number of warheads. The number of warheads attributed to each missile or bomber was the same for all missiles and bombers of that type. It did not recognize different loadings on individual delivery vehicles. This number was listed in an agreed database that the parties maintained during the life of the treaty. The parties then multiplied these warhead numbers by the number of deployed ballistic missiles and heavy bombers to determine the number of warheads that counted under the treaty's limits.

In most cases, the number of warheads attributed to each type of ICBM and SLBM was equal to the maximum number that missile had been tested with. START did, however, permit the parties to reduce the number of warheads attributed to some of their ballistic missiles through a process known as "downloading." When downloading missiles, a nation could remove a specified number of reentry vehicles from all the ICBMs at an ICBM base or from all the SLBMs in submarines at bases adjacent to a specified ocean.[9] They could then reduce the number of warheads attributed to those missiles in the database, and therefore, the number that counted under the treaty limits.

Unlike ballistic missiles, bombers counted as far fewer than the number of warheads they could carry. Bombers that were not equipped to carry long-range nuclear-armed cruise missiles counted as one warhead, even though they could carry 16 or more bombs and short-range missiles. U.S. bombers that were equipped to carry long-range nuclear-armed cruise missiles counted as 10 warheads, even though they could carry up to 20 cruise missiles. Soviet bombers that were equipped to carry long-range nuclear-armed cruise missiles counted as 8 warheads, even though they could carry up to 16 cruise missiles. These numbers were then multiplied by the numbers of deployed heavy bombers in each category to determine the number of warheads that would count under the treaty limits.

In contrast with START, the Moscow Treaty did not contain any definitions or counting rules to calculate the number of warheads that counted under the treaty limit. Its text indicated that it limited deployed strategic warheads, but the United States and Russia could each determine its own definition of this term. The United States counted "operationally deployed" strategic nuclear warheads and included both warheads on deployed ballistic missiles and bomber weapons stored near deployed bombers at their bases. Russia, in contrast, did not count any bomber weapons under its total, as these weapons were not actually deployed on any bombers. Moreover, because the Moscow Treaty did not contain any sublimits on warheads deployed on different categories of delivery vehicles, the two parties only had to calculate an aggregate total for their deployed warheads. In addition, while they exchanged data under START on the numbers of accountable

---

[9] A reentry vehicle is a cone-shaped container that holds a warhead to protect it from heat and other stresses when it reenters the Earth's atmosphere.

launchers and warheads every six months, they only had to report the number of warheads they counted under the Moscow Treaty once, on December 31, 2012, at the end of the treaty's implementation period.

Like START, the New START Treaty contains definitions and counting rules that will help the parties calculate the number of warheads that count under the treaty limits. For ballistic missiles, these rules follow the precedent set in the Moscow Treaty and count only the actual number of warheads on deployed delivery vehicles. For bombers, however, these rules follow the precedent set in START and attribute a fixed number of warheads to each heavy bomber.

Article III of the New START Treaty states that "for ICBMs and SLBMs, the number of warheads shall be the number of reentry vehicles emplaced on deployed ICBMs and on deployed SLBMs." Missiles will not count as if they carried the maximum number of warheads tested on that type of missile. Each missile will have its own warhead number and that number can change during the life of the treaty. The parties will not, however, visit each missile to count and calculate the total number of warheads in the force. The New START database will list total number of warheads deployed on all deployed launchers. The parties will then have the opportunity, 10 times each year, to inspect one missile or three bombers selected at random. At the start of these inspections, before the inspecting party chooses a missile or bomber to view, the inspected party will provide a list of the number of warheads on each missile or bomber at the inspected base. The inspecting party will then choose a missile at random, and confirm that the number listed in the database is accurate. This is designed to deter the deployment of extra warheads by creating the possibility that a missile with extra warheads might be chosen for an inspection.

As was the case under START, this inspection process will not provide the parties with the means to visually inspect and count all the deployed warheads carried on deployed missiles. Under START, this number was calculated by counting launchers and multiplying by an attributed number of warheads. Under New START, as was the case in the Moscow Treaty, each side will simply declare its number of total deployed warheads and include that number in the treaty data base. Unlike the Moscow Treaty, however, the parties will provide and update these numbers every six months during the life of the treaty, rather than just once at the end of the treaty.

Under the New START Treaty, each deployed heavy bomber equipped with nuclear armaments will count as one nuclear warhead. This is true whether the bomber is equipped to carry cruise missiles or gravity bombs. Neither the United States nor Russia deploys nuclear weapons on their bombers on a day-to-day basis. Because the treaty is supposed to count, and reduce, actual warheads carried by deployed delivery vehicles, the bomber weapons that are not deployed on a day-to-day basis are excluded. In addition, because the parties will use on-site inspections to confirm the actual number of deployed warheads on deployed delivery vehicles, and the bombers will have no warheads on them during inspections, the parties needed to come up with an arbitrary number to assign to the bombers. That number is one.

Conversion and Elimination

According to New START, ICBM launchers, SLBM launchers, and heavy bombers equipped to carry nuclear armaments shall continue to count under the treaty limits until they are converted or eliminated according to the provisions described in the treaty's Protocol. These provisions are far less demanding than those in the original START Treaty and will provide the United States and Russia with far more flexibility in determining how to reduce their forces to meet the treaty limits.

ICBM Launchers

Under START, ICBM launchers were "destroyed by excavation to a depth of no less than eight meters, or by explosion to a depth of no less than six meters." If missiles were removed from silos, and the silos were not eliminated in this fashion, then the silos still counted as if they held a deployed missile and as if the deployed missile carried the attributed number of warheads.

New START lists three ways in which the parties may eliminate ICBM silo launchers. It states that silo launchers "shall be destroyed by excavating them to a depth of no less than eight meters or by explosion to a depth of no less than six meters." It also indicates that the silos can be "completely filled with debris resulting from demolition of infrastructure, and with earth or gravel." Finally, it indicates the party carrying out the elimination can develop other procedures to eliminate its silos. It may have to demonstrate this elimination alternative to the other party, but that party cannot dispute or deny the use of that method.

Hence, instead of blowing up the silos, digging them out of the ground, of filling them with dirt, the parties to the treaty might simply choose to disable the silo, using measures it identifies itself, so that it can no longer launch a missile. This could be far less costly and destructive than the procedures mandated under START, and would help both nations eliminate some silos that have stood empty for years while continuing to count under the old START Treaty. For the United States, this would include the 50 silos that held Peacekeeper missiles until 2005 and the 50 silos that held Minuteman III missiles until 2008. The United States has never destroyed these silos, so they continued to count under START. It can now disable theses silos without destroying them, and remove them from its tally of launchers under the New START Treaty.

Mobile ICBM launchers

Under START, the elimination process for launchers for road-mobile ICBMs required that "the erector-launcher mechanism and leveling supports shall be removed from the launcher chassis" and that "the framework of the erector-launcher mechanism on which the ICBM is mounted and erected shall be cut at locations that are not assembly joints into two pieces of approximately equal size." It also required that the missile launch support equipment be removed from the launcher chassis, and that the "mountings of the erector-launcher mechanism and of the launcher leveling supports shall be cut off the launcher chassis" and cut into two pieces of approximately equal size. START also required that 0.78 meters of the launcher chassis be cut off and cut into two parts, so that the chassis would be too short to support mobile ICBMs.

Under New START, the elimination process for launchers for road mobile ICBMs is far more simple and far less destructive. As was the case under START, the elimination "shall be carried out by cutting the erector-launcher mechanism, leveling supports, and mountings of the erector-launcher mechanism from the launcher chassis and by removing the missile launch support equipment ... from the launcher chassis." But neither the framework nor the chassis itself have to be cut into pieces. If the chassis is going to be used "at a declared facility for purposes not inconsistent with the Treaty" the surfaces of the vehicle that will be visible to national technical means of verification must be painted a different color or pattern than those surfaces on a deployed mobile ICBM launcher.

SLBM Launchers

Under START, the SLBM launch tubes were considered to be eliminated when the entire missile section was removed from the submarine; or when "the missile launch tubes, and all elements of their reinforcement, including hull liners and segments of circular structural members between the missile launch tubes, as well as the entire portion of the pressure hull, the entire portion of the outer hull, and the entire portion of the superstructure through which all the missile launch tubes pass and that contain all the missile launch-tube penetrations" were removed from the submarine. The missile launch tubes then had to "be cut into two pieces of approximately equal size."

Under New START, SLBM launch tubes can be eliminated "by removing all missile launch tube hatches, their associated superstructure fairings, and, if applicable, gas generators." In other words, the missile section of the submarine and the individual launch tubes can remain in place in the submarine, and cease to count under the treaty limits, if they are altered so that they can no longer launch ballistic missiles. Moreover, according to the Ninth Agreed Statement in the New START Protocol, SLBM launch tubes that have been converted in accordance with this procedure and are "incapable of launching SLBMs may simultaneously be located on a ballistic missile submarine" with launch tubes that are still capable of launching SLBMs. After a party completes this type of conversion, it "shall conduct a one-time exhibition of a converted launcher and an SLBM launcher that has not been converted" to demonstrate, to the other party, "the distinguishing features of a converted launcher and an SLBM launcher that has not been converted."

Under START, the United States had to essentially destroy an entire submarine to remove its launch tubes from accountability under the treaty limits. With these provisions in New START, the United States can not only convert ballistic missile submarines to other uses without destroying their missile tubes and missile compartments, it can also reduce the number of accountable deployed SLBM launchers on ballistic missile submarines that continue to carry nuclear-armed SLBMs. These provisions will provide the United States a great deal of flexibility when it determines the structure of its nuclear forces under New START.

During the past decade, the United States has converted four of its Trident ballistic missile submarines so that they no longer carry ballistic missiles but now carry conventional cruise missiles and other types of weapons. These are now known as SSGNs. Because the United States did not remove the missile compartment from these submarines, they continued to count as if they carried 24 Trident missiles, with 8 warheads per missile, under the old START Treaty. These submarines will not count under the New START Treaty.

In the Second Agreed Statement in the New START Protocol, the United States has agreed that, "no later than three years after entry into force of the Treaty, the United States of America shall conduct an initial one-time exhibition of each of these four SSGNs. The purpose of such exhibitions shall be to confirm that the launchers on such submarines are incapable of launching SLBMs." Moreover, if an SSGN is located at an SSBN base when a Russian inspection team visits that base, the inspection team will have the right to inspect the SSGN again to confirm that the launchers have not been converted back to carry SLBMs. Russia can conduct six of these re-inspections during the life of the treaty, but no more than two inspections of any one of the SSGNs.

Heavy Bombers

Under START, heavy bombers were eliminated by having the tail section cut off of the fuselage at a location that obviously was not an assembly joint; having the wings separated from the fuselage at any location by any method; and having the remainder of the fuselage cut into two pieces, with the cut occurring in the area where the wings were attached to the fuselage, but at a location obviously not an assembly joint.

START also allowed the parties to remove heavy bombers from treaty accountability by converting them to heavy bombers that were not equipped to carry nuclear armaments. According to the elimination and conversion Protocol in START, this could be done by modifying all weapons bays and by removing or modifying the external attachment joints for either long-range nuclear ALCMs or other nuclear armaments that the bombers were equipped to carry.

The elimination procedure for heavy bombers has also been simplified under New START. To eliminate bombers, the parties must cut "a wing or tail section from the fuselage at locations obviously not assembly joints," *or* cut "the fuselage into two parts at a location obviously not an assembly joint." It no longer has to remove the wings from the fuselage. In addition, to convert a bomber counted under the treaty to a heavy bomber no longer equipped to carry nuclear armaments, the parties can either modify the weapons bays and external attachments for pylons so that they can not carry nuclear armaments, or modify all internal and external launcher assemblies so that they can not carry nuclear armaments, or develop any other procedure to carry out the conversion. As was the case with the conversion and elimination of missile launchers, the party may have to demonstrate its conversion procedure, but the other party does not have the right to object or reject the procedure.

The United States no longer equips its B-1 bombers with nuclear weapons, and has no plans to do so in the future. It has not, however, converted these bombers to non-nuclear heavy bombers using the procedures outlined in START. As a result, they continued to count as one delivery vehicle and one warhead under the counting rules in START. The United States does not, however, want to count these bombers under the New START Treaty. As a result, in the First Agreed Statement, the United States and Russia agreed, during the first year that the treaty is in force, the United States will conduct a "one-time exhibition" to demonstrate to Russia that these bombers are no longer equipped to carry nuclear weapons. The bombers that no longer carry nuclear weapons will have a "distinguishing feature" that will be recorded in the treaty database and will be evident on all B-1 bombers that are no longer equipped to carry nuclear weapons. After all the B-1 bombers have been converted in this manner, they will no longer count against the limits in the New START Treaty.

Mobile ICBMs

Mobile ICBMs in START

Mobile ICBMs became an issue in the original START negotiations in the mid-1980s, as the Soviet Union began to deploy a single warhead road-mobile ICBM, the SS-25, and a 10-warhead rail-mobile ICBM, the SS-24.[10] The United States initially proposed that START ban mobile

---

[10] In 1987, the United States began to develop its own mobile ICBM, the 10-warhead MX (Peacekeeper) missile and it (continued...)

ICBMs because the United States would not be able to locate or target these systems during a conflict. Some also questioned whether the United States would be able to monitor Soviet mobile ICBM deployments well enough to count the missiles and verify Soviet compliance with the limits in START. Some also argued that the Soviet Union might be able to stockpile hidden missiles and launchers, and to reload mobile ICBM launchers during a conflict because the United States could not target and destroy them.

The Soviet Union refused to ban mobile ICBMs. As a result, START limited the United States and Soviet Union to 1,100 warheads on mobile ICBMs. The treaty also limited the numbers of nondeployed missiles and nondeployed launchers for mobile ICBMs. Each side could retain 250 missiles and 110 launchers for mobile ICBMs, with no more than 125 missiles and 18 launchers for rail mobile ICBMs. This did not eliminate the risk of "breakout," which refers to the rapid addition of stored missiles to the deployed force, but it did limit the magnitude of the breakout potential and the number of missiles that the Soviet Union could "reload" on deployed launchers during a conflict.

START also contained a number of complementary, and sometimes overlapping, monitoring mechanisms that were designed to help the parties keep track of the numbers and locations of permitted missiles.[11] Each side could monitor the final assembly facility for the missiles to count them as they entered the force.[12] The parties also agreed to record the serial numbers, referred to in the treaty as "unique identifiers," for the mobile ICBMs, and to list these numbers in the treaty's database. These numbers were used to help track and identify permitted missiles because the parties could check the serial numbers during on-site inspections to confirm that the missiles they encountered were those that they expected to see at the facility during the inspection. The parties also had to provide notifications when mobile ICBMs moved between permitted facilities and when mobile ICBMs moved out of their main operating bases for an exercise. These notifications were designed to complicate efforts to move extra, hidden missiles into the deployed force. Finally, missiles and launchers removed from the force had to be eliminated according to specific procedures outlined in the treaty. This not only helped the parties keep an accurate count of the deployed missiles, but served as a further deterrent to efforts to hide extra missiles outside the treaty regime.

Mobile ICBMs in New START

The New START Treaty contains many limits and restrictions that will affect Russia's force of mobile ICBMs, but it does not single them out with many of the additional constraints that were contained in START. Russia pressed for an easing of the restrictions on mobile ICBMs in New START, in part because these restrictions were one sided and only affected Russian forces. But Russian officials also noted, and the United States agreed, that mobile ICBMs could enhance the

---

(...continued)

continued to explore mobile basing for the new single warhead small ICBM. Although it eventually deployed the Peacekeeper missile in fixed silos, the parties considered it to be a mobile ICBM under the terms of START.

[11] For more information on the monitoring regime in START, see CRS Report R41201, *Monitoring and Verification in Arms Control*, by Amy F. Woolf.

[12] The perimeter/portal continuous monitoring systems (PPCMS) consisted of fences surrounding the entire perimeter of the facility and one restricted portal through which all vehicles large enough to carry items limited by the treaty (such as the first stage of a mobile ICBM) had to pass. The portal contained scales and other measuring devices that the countries could use to determine whether the vehicle carried an item limited by the treaty.

survivability of Russia's nuclear forces, and therefore strengthen strategic stability under the new treaty.

The United States was also willing to relax the restrictions on mobile ICBMs because it is far less concerned about Russia's ability to break out of the treaty limits than it was in the 1980s. After 15 years of START implementation, the United States has far more confidence in its knowledge of the number of deployed and nondeployed Russian mobile ICBMs, as it kept count of these missiles as they entered and left the Russian force during START. There is also far less concern about Russia stockpiling extra missiles while New START is in force. During the 1980s, the Soviet Union produced dozens of new missiles each year; Russia now adds fewer than 10 missiles to its force each year.[13] Some estimates indicate that, with this level of production, Russia will find it difficult to retain the 700 deployed missiles permitted by the treaty. In such a circumstance, it would have neither the need nor the ability to stockpile and hide extra missiles. Moreover, where the United States was once concerned about Russia's ability to reload its mobile launchers with spare missiles, after launching the first missiles during a conflict, this scenario no longer seems credible. It would mean that Russia maintained the ability to send extra missiles and the equipment needed to load them on launchers out on patrol with its deployed systems and that it could load these missile quickly, in the field, in the midst of a nuclear war, with U.S. weapons falling all around. Yet, Russia has not practiced or exercised this capability and it is hard to imagine that it would try it, for the first time, in the midst of a nuclear war.

The New START Treaty does not contain a sublimit on mobile ICBMs or their warheads. It also does not contain any limits on the number of nondeployed mobile ICBMs or the number of nondeployed mobile ICBM launchers. These launchers and warheads will, however, count under the aggregate limits set by the treaty, including the limit of 800 deployed and nondeployed launchers. As a result, the United States will still need to count the number of mobile ICBMs in Russia's force.

New START will not permit perimeter and portal monitoring at missile assembly facilities. The parties must, however, provide notification at least 48 hours before the time when solid-fuel ICBMs and solid-fuel SLBMs leave the production facilities. Moreover, the parties will continue to list the serial numbers, or unique identifiers, for mobile ICBMs in the shared database.[14]

New START limits the locations of mobile ICBMs and their launchers, both to help the United States keep track of the missiles covered by the treaty and to deter Russian efforts to hide extra missiles away from the deployed force. Deployed mobile ICBMs and their launchers must be located only at ICBM bases. All nondeployed launchers for mobile ICBMs must be located at "production facilities, ICBM loading facilities, repair facilities, storage facilities, conversion or elimination facilities, training facilities, test ranges, and space launch facilities." The locations of nondeployed mobile ICBMs are also limited to loading facilities, maintenance facilities, repair facilities, storage facilities, conversion or elimination facilities test ranges, space launch facilities, and production facilities. Some of these facilities may be at bases for operational mobile ICBMs, but, in that case, the nondeployed missiles must remain in the designated facility and cannot be located in deployment areas.

---

[13] According to one U.S. inspector, monitoring at Votkinsk "was very monotonous. We could have months go by without inspecting a missile." See Elaine M. Grossman, "U.S. Treaty-Monitoring Presence at Russian Missile Plant Winding Down," *Global Security Newswire*, November 20, 2009.

[14] In START, the parties recorded unique identifiers only for mobile ICBMs. In new START, the parties will record these numbers for all ICBMs, SLBMs, and heavy bombers covered by the limits in Treaty.

Moreover, when deployed or nondeployed missiles or launchers move from one facility to another, the parties will have to update the database so each facility contains a complete list of each item located at that facility, and of the unique identifier associated with each item. Then, according to the Protocol to the Treaty, "inspectors shall have the right to read the unique identifiers on all designated deployed ICBMs or designated deployed SLBMs, non-deployed ICBMs, non-deployed SLBMs, and designated heavy bombers that are located at the inspection site."[15] Hence, the parties will have the opportunity to confirm that items located at the facilities are supposed to be there.

This is designed not only to increase transparency and understanding while the treaty is in force, but also to discourage efforts to hide extra missiles and break out of the treaty limits. The treaty does not limit the number of nondeployed missiles, but it does provide the United States with continuous information about their locations and the opportunity, during on-site inspections, to confirm that these missiles are not mixed into the deployed force. Moreover, the number of nondeployed launchers for these missiles is limited, under the 800 limit on deployed and nondeployed launchers. So, even if Russia did accumulate a stock of nondeployed missiles, the number that it could add to its force in a relatively short amount of time would be limited.

Some have questioned whether Russia might use these stored mobile ICBMs to break out of the treaty by deploying them on mobile launchers that are not limited by the treaty. Specifically, they have questioned whether the New START Treaty would count rail-mobile ICBMs, and, if not, whether Russia could develop and deploy enough of these launchers to gain a military advantage over the United States.[16] This concern derives from the definition of mobile launcher in the paragraph 45 of the Protocol to the Treaty, which indicates that a mobile launcher is "an erector-launcher mechanism for launching ICBMs and the *self-propelled* device on which it is mounted [emphasis added]." This definition clearly captures road-mobile launchers, such as those that Russia uses for its SS-25 and SS-27 missiles, because the transporters for these missiles are self-propelled. But a rail car that carried an erector-launcher for an ICBM would not be self-propelled; it would be propelled by the train's locomotive.

Others, however, point to several provisions in the treaty that indicate that rail-mobile launchers of ICBMs would count under the treaty limits. First, they note that the treaty limits all deployed and nondeployed ICBM launchers. It defines ICBM launcher, in paragraph 28 of the Protocol to the Treaty, as "a device intended or used to contain, prepare for launch, and launch an ICBM." Any erector-launcher for ICBMs would be covered by this definition, regardless of whether it was deployed on a fixed site, on a road-mobile transporter, or on a railcar.

Moreover, the article-by-article analysis of the treaty specifically states that "all of the defined terms are used in at least one place elsewhere in the Treaty documents." Article III, paragraph 8 of the treaty lists the current types of weapons deployed by each side and notes that these all count against the limits. It does not list any missiles deployed on rail-mobile launchers, and, therefore, the Protocol does not define rail-mobile launchers, because Russia no longer deploys any missiles on rail-mobile launchers. It had deployed SS-24 missiles on such launchers during

---

[15] http://www.state.gov/documents/organization/140047.pdf.

[16]See, for example, Christopher Ford, "Does New START Fumble Reloads and Rail-Mobile ICBMs?" New Paradigms Forum, April 26, 2010, http://02e18f7.netsolhost.com/New_Paradigms_Forum/Nuclear_Weapons/Entries/2010/4/ 26_New_START_Fumbles_Missile_REloads_and_Rail-Mobile_ICBMs html.

---

the 1980s and 1990s, but these were all retired in the past decade, and the last operating base for these missiles and railcars was closed in 2007.[17]

The treaty would not prohibit Russia from deploying these types of systems again in the future. Article V specifically states that "modernization and replacement of strategic offensive arms may be carried out." However, the second paragraph of this article indicates that, "when a party believes a new kind of strategic offensive arms is emerging, that party shall have the right to raise the question of such a strategic offensive arm for consideration in the Bilateral Consultative Commission." Section six of the Protocol to the Treaty, which describes the Bilateral Consultative Commission, states that this body should "resolve questions related to the applicability of provisions of the treaty to a new kind of strategic offensive arm." In addition, Article XV of the treaty states that "if it becomes necessary to make changes in the Protocol ... that do not affect the substantive rights or obligations under this Treaty," the parties can use the BCC to reach agreement on these changes without amending the treaty. Hence, if Russia were to deploy ICBMs on rail-mobile launchers, the parties could modify the definition to "mobile launcher" to confirm that these weapons count under the treaty limits.

New START does not define rail-mobile launchers for ICBMs because neither the United States nor Russia currently deploys theses systems and the treaty does not specifically prohibit their deployment in the future. If, however, either party installs an erector-launcher for an ICBM on a rail car, that launcher would count under the treaty limits, and the new type of strategic arm, represented by the launcher on a railcar, would be covered by the limits in the treaty. The parties would then use the BCC to determine which of the monitoring provisions and elimination and conversion rules applied to that type of weapons system.

Monitoring and Verification[18]

The original START Treaty included a comprehensive and overlapping set of provisions that was designed to allow the United States and Soviet Union to collect a wide range of data on their forces and activities and to determine whether the forces and activities were consistent with the limits in the treaty. While each party would collect most of this information with its own satellites and remote sensing equipment—known as national technical means of verification (NTM)—the treaty also called for the extensive exchange of data detailing the numbers and locations of affected weapons, numerous types of on-site inspections, notifications, exhibitions, and continuous monitoring at assembly facilities for mobile ICBMs. Further, in START, the parties agreed that they would not encrypt or otherwise deny access to the telemetry generated during missile flight tests, so that the other side could record this data and use it in evaluating the capabilities of missile systems.

The New START Treaty contains a monitoring and verification regime that resembles the regime in START, in that its text contains detailed definitions of items limited by the treaty, provisions governing the use of NTM to gather data on each side's forces and activities, an extensive database that identifies the numbers, types, and locations of items limited by the treaty, provisions requiring notifications about items limited by the treaty, and inspections allowing the parties to

---

[17] Pavel Podvig, *New START on Rail-Mobile ICBMs and Reloads*, April 29, 2010, http://russianforces.org/blog/2010/04/new_start_on_rail-mobile_icbms.shtml.

[18] For more information on the monitoring and verification regime in new START, see CRS Report R41201, *Monitoring and Verification in Arms Control*, by Amy F. Woolf.

confirm information shared during data exchanges. At the same time, the verification regime has been streamlined to make it less costly and complex than the regime in START. It also has been adjusted to reflect the limits in New START and the current circumstances in the relationship between the United States in Russia. In particular, it focuses on maintaining transparency, cooperation, and openness, as well as on deterring and detecting potential violations.

Under New START, the United States and Russia will continue to rely on their NTM to collect information about the numbers and locations of their strategic forces. They may also broadcast and exchange telemetry—the data generated during missile flight tests—up to five times each year. They do not need this data to monitor compliance with any particular limits in New START, but the telemetry exchange will provide some transparency into the capabilities of their systems.[19] The parties will also exchange a vast amount of data about those forces, specifying not only their distinguishing characteristics, but also their precise locations and the number of warheads deployed on each deployed delivery vehicle. They will notify each other, and update the database, whenever they move forces between declared facilities. The treaty also requires the parties to display their forces, and allows each side to participate in exhibitions, to confirm information listed in the database.

New START will also permit the parties to conduct up to 18 short-notice on-site inspections each year. These inspections will begin in early April 2011, 60 days after the treaty enters into force. These inspections can occur at facilities that house both deployed and nondeployed launchers and missiles. The treaty divides these into Type One inspections and Type Two inspections. Each side can conduct up to 10 Type One inspections and up to eight Type Two inspections. Moreover, during each Type One inspection, the parties will be able to perform two different types of inspection activities—these are essentially equivalent to the data update inspections and reentry vehicle inspections in the original START Treaty. As a result, the 18 short-notice inspections permitted under New START are essentially equivalent to the 28 short-notice inspections permitted under START.

Type One Inspections

Type One inspections are those that will occur at ICBM bases, submarine bases, and air bases that house deployed or nondeployed launchers, missiles, and bombers. The parties will use these inspections "to confirm the accuracy of declared data on the numbers and types of deployed and non-deployed strategic offensive arms subject to this treaty. During Type One inspections, the parties will also be able to confirm that the number of warheads located on deployed ICBMs and deployed SLBMs and the number of nuclear armaments located on deployed heavy bombers" are consistent with the numbers listed in the treaty database.

The inspections used to confirm the number of deployed warheads in New START will be distinctly different from the inspections in START because the counting rules for ballistic missiles have changed. Under START, the treaty database listed the number of warheads *attributed* to a type of missile, and each missile of that type counted as the same number of warheads. The parties then inspected the missiles to confirm that the number of warheads on a particular missile did not exceed the number attributed to that type of missile. The database in New START will list the aggregate number of warheads deployed on all the missiles at a given base, but before

---

[19] U.S. State Department, Bureau of Verification, Compliance and Implementation, *Telemetry*, Fact Sheet, Washington, DC, April 8, 2010, http://www.state.gov/t/vci/rls/139904 htm.

beginning a Type One inspection, the team will receive a briefing on the actual number of warheads deployed *on each missile* at the base. During the inspections, the parties will have the right to designate one ICBM or one SLBM for inspection, and, when inspecting that missile, the parties will be able to count the actual number of reentry vehicles deployed on the missile to confirm that it equals the number provided for that particular missile prior to the inspection. The inspected party can cover the reentry vehicles to protect information not related to the number of warheads, but the party must use covers that allow the inspectors to identify the actual number of warheads on the missile.

Because these inspections will be random, and will occur on short notice, they provide the parties with a chance to detect an effort by the other party to deploy a missile with more than its listed number of warheads. As a result, the inspections may deter efforts to conceal extra warheads on the deployed force. These inspections, by allowing the parties to count the actual number of deployed warheads, also provide added transparency.

Type Two Inspections

Type Two inspections will occur at facilities that house non-deployed or converted launchers and missiles. These include "ICBM loading facilities; SLBM loading facilities; storage facilities for ICBMs, SLBMs, and mobile launchers of ICBMs; repair facilities for ICBMs, SLBMs, and mobile launchers of ICBMs; test ranges; and training facilities." The parties will use these inspections "to confirm the accuracy of declared technical characteristics and declared data, specified for such facilities, on the number and types of non-deployed ICBMs and non-deployed SLBMs, first stages of ICBMs and SLBMs, and nondeployed launchers of ICBMs." In addition, they can conduct these inspections at formerly declared facilities, "to confirm that such facilities are not being used for purposes inconsistent with this Treaty." They will also use Type II inspections to confirm that solid-fueled ICBMs, solid-fueled SLBMs, or mobile launchers of ICBMs have been eliminated according to treaty procedures.

Ballistic Missile Defense

Presidents Obama and Medvedev had agreed, when they met in April 2009, that the two nations would address Russia's concerns with U.S. missile defense programs in a separate forum from the negotiations on a New START Treaty.[20] However, during their meeting in Moscow in July 2010, Presidents Obama and Medvedev agreed that the treaty would contain a "provision on the interrelationship of strategic offensive arms and strategic defensive arms."[21] This statement, which appears in the preamble to New START, states that the parties recognize "the existence of the interrelationship between strategic offensive arms and strategic defensive arms, that this interrelationship will become more important as strategic nuclear arms are reduced, and that current strategic defensive arms do not undermine the viability and effectiveness of the strategic offensive arms of the parties."

---

[20] The White House, Office of the Press Secretary, *Joint Statement by President Dmitriy Medvedev of the Russian Federation and President Barack Obama of the United States of America*, April 1, 2009. http://www.whitehouse.gov/the_press_office/Joint-Statement-by-President-Dmitriy-Medvedev-of-the-Russian-Federation-and-President-Barack-Obama-of-the-United-States-of-America/.

[21] The White House, Office of the Press Secretary, Joint Understanding by Obama, Medvedev on Weapon Negotiations. July 8, 2009. http://www.america.gov/st/texttrans-english/2009/July/20090708154724xjsnommis0.7355005.html.

Russia and the United States each issued unilateral statements when they signed New START that clarified their positions on the relationship between New START and missile defenses. Russia stated that

> the Treaty can operate and be viable only if the United States of America refrains from developing its missile defense capabilities quantitatively or qualitatively. Consequently, the exceptional circumstances referred to in Article 14 of the Treaty include increasing the capabilities of the United States of America's missile defense system in such a way that threatens the potential of the strategic nuclear forces of the Russian Federation.[22]

In its statement, the United States stated that its

> missile defense systems are not intended to affect the strategic balance with Russia. The United States missile defense systems would be employed to defend the United States against limited missile launches, and to defend its deployed forces, allies and partners against regional threats. The United States intends to continue improving and deploying its missile defense systems in order to defend itself against limited attack and as part of our collaborative approach to strengthening stability in key regions.[23]

These statements do not impose any obligations on either the United States and Russia. As Senator Lugar indicated before New START was signed, these statements are, "in essence editorial opinions." Under Secretary of State Ellen Tauscher has also stated that "Russia's unilateral statement on missile defenses is not an integral part of the New START Treaty. It's not legally-binding. It won't constrain U.S. missile defense programs."[24] These statements also do not provide Russia with "veto power" over U.S. missile defense systems. Although Russia has said it may withdraw from the treaty if the U.S. missile defenses threaten "the potential of the strategic nuclear forces of the Russian Federation," the United States has no obligation to consult with Russia to confirm that its planned defenses do not cross this threshold. It may develop and deploy whatever defenses it chooses; Russia can then determine, for itself, whether those defenses affect its strategic nuclear forces and whether it thinks the threat to those forces justifies withdrawal from the treaty.

Article V, paragraph 3 of New START also mentions ballistic missile defense interceptors. It states that the parties cannot convert ICBM launchers and SLBM launchers to launchers for missile defense interceptors and that they cannot convert launchers of missile defense interceptors to launchers for ICBMs and SLBMs. At the same time, the treaty makes it clear that the five ICBM silos at Vandenberg Air Force Base that have already been converted to carry missile defense interceptors are not affected by this prohibition. It states that "this provision shall not apply to ICBM launchers that were converted prior to signature of this Treaty for placement of missile defense interceptors therein."

This provision is designed to address Russian concerns about the U.S. ability to "break out" of the treaty by placing ICBMs in silos that had held missile defense interceptors or by converting ICBM silos to missile interceptor silos then quickly reversing that conversion to add offensive

---

[22] Article 14, following the form of most previous arms control treaties, indicates that each party shall have the right to withdraw from the Treaty if it decides that extraordinary events related to the subject of the Treaty have jeopardized its supreme national interests. For the Russian statement, see http://eng kremlin ru/text/docs/2010/04/225214.shtml

[23] http://www.state.gov/documents/organization/140406.pdf.

[24] Under Secretary of State Ellen Tauscher, *The Case for New START Ratification*, Atlantic Council Panel Discussion, April 21, 2010. http://www.state.gov/t/us/140633 htm.

missiles to its forces with little warning. Russia began to express this concern after the United States converted the five ICBM silos at Vandenberg for missile defense interceptors. It initially sought to reverse this conversion, or at least to count the silos under the New START limits. The United States refused, but, in exchange for Russia accepting that the five converted silos would not count under New START, the United States agreed that it would not convert additional silos.

The provision will also protect U.S. missile defense interceptors from the START inspection regime. If the parties were permitted to convert missile defense silos to ICBM silos, they would also have been able to visit and inspect those silos to confirm that they did not hold missiles limited by the treaty. The ban on such conversions means that this type of inspection are not only unnecessary, but also not permitted.

The Obama Administration has stated on many occasions that the New START Treaty does not contain any provisions that limit the numbers or capabilities of current or planned U.S. ballistic missile defense systems.[25] The ban on launcher conversion does not alter this conclusion because the United States has no plans to use any additional ICBM launchers or any SLBM launchers to hold missile defense interceptors. It is constructing new launchers for its missile defense systems. Some have questioned, however, whether the ban on silo conversion may limit missile defenses in the future, particularly if the United States wanted to respond to an emerging missile threat by quickly expanding its numbers of missile defense interceptors.[26]

General Jim Jones, President Obama's National Security Adviser, has stated that this provision is a "limit in theory, but not in reality."[27] It is not just that the United States has no plans to convert ICBM silos to missile defense interceptor silos, it is that it would be quicker and less expensive for the United States to build new silos for missile defense interceptors than to remove the ICBMs and all their equipment, reconfigure the silo, and install all the equipment for the missile defense interceptors. Moreover, given that the missile defense interceptor launched from the central United States, where U.S. ICBM silos are located, would drop debris on U.S. territory, the United States might prefer to locate its missile defense interceptors in new launchers near the U.S. coast.

General Patrick O'Reilly, the Director of the Missile Defense Agency, has also stated that his agency "never had a plan to convert additional ICBM silos at Vandenberg and intends to hedge against increased BMDS [ballistic missile defense system] requirements by completing construction of Missile Field 2 at Fort Greely. Moreover, we determined that if more interceptors were to be added at Vandenberg AFB, it would be less expensive to build a new GBI [ground-based interceptor] missile field (which is not prohibited by the treaty)."[28] He went on to note that "some time ago we examined the concept of launching missile defense interceptors from submarines and found it an unattractive and extremely expensive option." Putting missile defense interceptors in SLBM launchers would undermine the primary mission of the submarine, which is designed to patrol deeply and quietly to remain invulnerable to attack, by requiring it to remain in one place near the surface while it sought to track and engage attacking missiles.

---

[25] The White House, Office of the Press Secretary, *Key Facts About the New START Treaty*, Washington, DC, March 26, 2010, http://www.whitehouse.gov/the-press-office/key-facts-about-new-start-treaty. See, also, the remarks of Under Secretary of State Ellen Tauscher at Atlantic Council Panel Discussion on April 21, 2010. http://www.state.gov/t/us/140633 htm.

[26] "Stopping Missile Defense?," *Wall Street Journal*, April 17, 2010, p. A12.

[27] James L. Jones, "New START Treaty Won't Limit Missile Defenses," *Wall Street Journal*, April 20, 2010.

[28] U.S. Congress, House Armed Services, Strategic Forces, *President Obama's Fiscal 2011 Budget Request for the Missile Defense and Ballistic Missile Review Programs*, Hearing, 111th Cong., 2nd sess., April 14, 2010.

Conventional Long-Range Strike

During their summit meeting in July 2009, Presidents Obama and Medvedev agreed that the New START Treaty would contain "a provision on the impact of intercontinental ballistic missiles and submarine-launched ballistic missiles in a non-nuclear configuration on strategic stability." This statement, which is in the preamble to the treaty, simply states that the parties are "mindful of the impact of conventionally armed ICBMs and SLBMs on strategic stability."

During the negotiations on New START, Russia voiced concerns about U.S. plans to deploy conventional warheads on ballistic missiles that now carry nuclear warheads.[29] Russian officials have argued that these weapons could upset stability for several reasons. First, even if Russia were not the target of an attack with these missiles, it might not know whether the missile carried a nuclear warhead or a conventional warhead, or whether it was headed towards a target in Russia. Moreover, ballistic missiles armed with conventional warheads could destroy significant targets in Russia and, therefore, they might provide the United States with the ability to attack such targets, with little warning, without resorting to nuclear weapons. Finally, some argued that the United States might replace the conventional warheads with nuclear warheads to exceed the limits in a treaty.

Russia initially sought to include a provision in New START that would ban the deployment of conventional warheads on strategic ballistic missiles. The United States rejected this proposal. It is seeking this capability as a way to attack targets around the world promptly, and does not envision using these weapons against Russia. As a result, as the White House noted in its Fact Sheet on New START, "the Treaty does not contain any constraints on ... current or planned United States long-range conventional strike capabilities."[30] However, if the United States deploys conventional warheads on missiles that are covered by the limits in START, the warheads on these missiles will count under the treaty limit on deployed warheads. Because the United States expects to deploy very small numbers of these systems, this trade-off would not have a significant effect on U.S. nuclear capabilities.[31] Moreover, if the United States deploys conventional warheads on new types of long-range strike systems that are currently under development, these systems would not count under or be affected by the limits in New START.

U.S. and Russian Forces Under New START

U.S. Forces

According to the 2010 Nuclear Posture Review (NPR), which was released by DOD on April 6, 2010,[32] the United States will maintain a triad of ICBMs, SLBMs, and heavy bombers under New

---

[29] For information about the issues associated with the potential deployment of conventional warheads on ballistic missiles see CRS Report R41464, *Conventional Prompt Global Strike and Long-Range Ballistic Missiles: Background and Issues*, by Amy F. Woolf. See, also David E. Sanger and Thom Shanker, "U.S. Faces Choice of New Weapons for Fast Strikes," *New York Times*, April 23, 2010.

[30] The White House, Office of the Press Secretary, *Key Facts About the New START Treaty*, Washington, DC, March 26, 2010, http://www.whitehouse.gov/the-press-office/key-facts-about-new-start-treaty.

[31] U.S. State Department, Bureau of Verification, Compliance, and Implementation, *Conventional Prompt Global Strike*, Fact Sheet, Washington, DC, April 8, 2010, http://www.state.gov/t/vci/rls/139913.htm.

[32] U.S. Department of Defense, *Nuclear Posture Review*, Washington, DC, April 6, 2010, pp. 19-25.

START. The NPR did not specify how many ICBMs would remain in the force, but indicated that each would be deployed with only one warhead. It also indicated that the United States would, initially at least, retain 14 Trident submarines. It might, however, reduce its fleet to 12 submarines after 2015. The NPR did not indicate whether the Trident submarines would continue to be deployed with 24 missiles on each submarine, or if the Navy would eliminate some of the launchers on operational submarines in accordance with the treaty's Ninth Agreed Statement. Finally, the NPR indicated that the United States would convert some of its 76 dual-capable B-52 bombers to a conventional-only role.

The Administration clarified its plans for U.S. forces under New START in the 1251 plan that it submitted to the Senate with the treaty documents on May 13, 2010.[33] This plan indicated that the United States would eliminate at least 30 ICBM silos, retaining a force of up to 420 launchers under the treaty limits. It would also retain 14 Trident submarines, but each submarine would contain only 20 launchers, and two of the submarines would be in overhaul at any time, so 40 of the launchers would not count under the limit on deployed launchers. In addition, the report indicated that the United States would retain up to 60 bombers equipped for nuclear weapons, including all 18 B-2 bombers in the current force.

This force includes up to 720 deployed ICBMs, SLBMs, and heavy bombers, a number that exceeds the 700 deployed missiles and bombers permitted by the treaty. In a hearing before the Senate Armed Services Committee on June 17, 2010, Secretary of Defense Gates and Admiral Mullen acknowledged that the United States would have to make a small number of further reductions, or convert a small number of additional systems to non-deployed status, to meet the treaty limits. However, they noted that because the United States will have seven years to reduce its forces to these limits, they saw no reason to identify a final force structure at this point. Secretary Gates noted that DOD was considering a number of options for the final force structure, and would make a decision on this force structure after considering the international security environment and Russia's force structure in the treaty's later years.

Table 2, below, contains an estimated force structure of the United States prior to New START's entry into force; the current force structure, as of October 2011; and a potential force for the United States under New START that is consistent with the force outlined in the 1251 report. The force assumes, as the Administration has indicated, that the United States will retain a triad of ICBMs, SLBMs, and heavy bombers, and that it will reduce the number of deployed nuclear-armed B-52 bombers to meet the limits in New START. The table indicates that, under the treaty limit of 800 total launchers, the United States could reduce the number of launchers on its Trident submarines and retain up to 420 total Minuteman III missiles in its force. Some of the Minuteman III launchers would not hold ICBMs, and would, therefore, not count under the 700 limit for deployed launchers. The United States would adjust the number of warheads on deployed SLBMs to meet the treaty limit of 1,550 warheads.

The United States will not have to destroy many ICBM or SL BM launchers to reach the limits in New START. The treaty includes provisions that will allow the United States to exempt many of its existing nondeployed launchers, including 50 empty ICBM silos, 94 B-1 bombers, and 4 ballistic missile submarines that have been converted to carry cruise missiles, from the treaty limits. Moreover, as it reduces its deployed forces, the United States would not have to destroy

---

[33] Congress mandated that the President submit a report on this plan in Section 1251 of the FY2010 Defense Authorization Act. P.L. 111-84.

either ICBM or SLBM launchers to remove them from the treaty limits; it could deactivate them so that they could no longer launch ballistic missiles. Instead of eliminating missiles and launchers, the United States plans to reach the limits in New START by deploying its missiles with far fewer than the maximum number of warheads that each could be equipped to carry.

Table 2. U.S. Strategic Nuclear Forces Under New START

(Estimated current forces and potential New START forces)

	Estimated U.S. Forces, 2010		Current U.S. Forces, October 2011[a]			Potential Forces Under New START[b]		
	Deployed Launchers	Warheads	Total Launchers	Deployed Launchers	Warheads	Total Launchers	Deployed Launchers	Warheads
Minuteman III	450	500	506	448		420	400	400
Peacekeeper	0	0	51	0		0	0	0
Trident	336	1152	336	249		280	240	1090
B-52	76	300	130	114		74	42	42
B-2	18	200	20	11		18	18	18
Total	880	2152	1,043	822	1,790	792	700	1550

Source: CRS estimates.

a. U.S. Department of State, Bureau of State, Bureau of Arms Control, Verification, and Compliance, *New START Treaty Aggregate Numbers of Strategic Offensive Forces*, Fact Sheet, Washington, D.C., December 1, 2012, http://www.state.gov/documents/organization/178270.pdf. The Fact Sheet does not display warhead subtotals for each delivery system; it only includes an aggregate across the force.

b. This force assumes that the United States retains 14 Trident submarines, with two submarines in overhaul, but that each has only 20 deployed launchers.

Russian Forces

According to the most recent data exchange under the New START Treaty, Russia currently has 1,566 warheads on 516 deployed ICBMs, SLBMs, and heavy bombers, within a total of 871 deployed and nondeployed launchers.[34] It is currently retiring its older SS-25 mobile ICBMs, and replacing them with newer SS-27 ICBMs and the anticipated RS-24 ICBM. Unlike the SS-25 and SS-27, the RS-24 can reportedly carry up to 7 warheads.

Russia is also retiring many of its older ballistic missile submarines. It has several new Borey-class submarines under construction, and plans to deploy them with the new Bulava missile. The missile has, however, failed in most of its flight tests, so it is not known when Russia will deploy this new system.

Table 3, below, presents estimates of Russia's current force structure and potential forces that it might deploy under the New START Treaty. This table assumes that Russia's new RS-24 missile

---

[34] U.S. Department of State, Bureau of State, Bureau of Arms Control, Verification, and Compliance, *New START Treaty Aggregate Numbers of Strategic Offensive Forces*, Fact Sheet, Washington, D.C., December 1, 2012, http://www.state.gov/documents/organization/178270.pdf.

would carry 4 warheads. However, according to accounts in the Russian press this missile will carry "no fewer than 4" warheads. If each of these missiles were to carry 6-7 warheads, Russia could retain the 1,550 warheads permitted by the treaty. Moreover, the table assumes that Russia will eliminate most of its SS-18 ICBMs and all of its SS-19 ICBMs. It could retain some of these older missiles, both to increase the number of total and deployed launchers and to increase the number of deployed warheads.

Table 3 indicates that Russia will almost certainly deploy fewer than the permitted number of deployed and nondeployed launchers under New START. It currently has only 516 deployed launchers, and this number may decline to around 400 deployed and 444 total launchers. This would likely be true whether or not the treaty enters into force because Russia is eliminating older missiles as they age, and deploying newer missiles at a far slower pace than that needed to retain 700 deployed launchers. However, at the same time, Russia will have to reduce the number of warheads carried on its force to meet the treaty limits. As **Table 3** indicates, prior to implementation of New START, it had around 2,800 warheads on its strategic offensive forces, including many bomber weapons that will not count under the treaty. At the same time, because Russia will reduce its number of deployed launchers, it is likely that, under New START, Russia will deploy most of its missiles with the maximum number of warheads they are capable of carrying, so that it can retain the full quantity of 1,550 warheads.

Table 3. Russian Strategic Nuclear Forces Under New START

(Estimated current forces and potential New START forces)

	Estimated Forces 2010		Potential Forces under New START		
	Launchers	Warheads	Total Launchers	Deployed Launchers	Deployed Warheads
SS-18 ICBM	68	680	68	20	200
SS-19 ICBM	72	432	0	0	0
SS-25 (mobile)	180	180	0	0	0
SS-27 (mobile)	13	13	27	27	27
SS-27 (silo)	50	50	60	60	60
RS-24 (mobile)	0	0	85	85	340
SS-N-18 (Delta III SSBN)	64 (4 SSBNs)	192	0	0	0
SS-N-23 (Delta IV SSBN)	96 (6 SSBNs)	384	64 (4 SSBNs)	64	256
Bulava (Borey SSBN)	0	0	64 (4 SSBNs)	64	384
Blackjack Bomber	14	168	13	13	13
Bear Bomber	63	688	63	63	63
Total	620	2787	444	396	1335

Source: United States Department of State, Fact Sheet, START Aggregate Numbers of Strategic Offensive Arms, July 1, 2009; Nuclear Notebook: Russian Nuclear Forces, 2010," *Bulletin of the Atomic Scientists*, January/February 2010; Russian Nuclear Forces http://russianforces.org/.

Ratification

U.S. Ratification Process

The Obama Administration submitted the New START Treaty to the Senate on May 13, 2010. The treaty package included the treaty text, the Protocol, the Annexes, the Article-by-Article analysis prepared by the Administration, and the 1251 report on future plans and budgets for U.S. nuclear weapons required by Congress. It also included the text of the unilateral statements made by the United States and Russia when they signed the treaty. The Senate offered its advice and consent to the ratification of the treaty by voting on a Resolution of Ratification. The treaty's approval requires a vote of two-thirds of the Senate, or 67 Senators.

The Senate Foreign Relations Committee has held 12 hearings on the treaty. These began in April 2009, with testimony from former Secretaries of Defense William Perry and James Schlesinger. In total, the committee received testimony from more than 20 witnesses from both inside and outside the Obama Administration. It received testimony from current senior officials from the State Department, the Defense Department, and the Department of Energy, and from several former officials from past Administrations. The committee completed its hearing process in mid-July, after receiving a National Intelligence Estimate on the future of Russian forces and a report on the verifiability of the treaty.

The Senate Armed Services Committee held a total of eight hearings and briefings on the treaty. The Armed Services Committee heard testimony from Secretary of State Clinton, Secretary of Defense Gates, Secretary of Energy Chu, and Admiral Mullen on June 17, 2010. It also received testimony and briefings from other Administration officials and from experts from outside the government. The Intelligence Committee also held a closed hearing to discuss U.S. monitoring capabilities and the verifiability of the treaty.

The Senate Foreign Relations Committee held a business meeting to mark up the Resolution of Ratification for New START on September 16, 2010.[35] The committee began its consideration with a draft proposed by Senator Lugar, then addressed a number of amendments proposed by members of the committee. Both the Lugar draft and many of the proposed amendments addressed the members' concerns with U.S. missile defense programs, U.S. conventional prompt global strike capabilities, monitoring and verification, and Russian nonstrategic nuclear weapons. Most of these amendments were defeated, although the committee did modify and incorporate some into the resolution.[36]

The Senate Foreign Relations Committee approved the Resolution of Ratification by a vote of 14-4, and sent the resolution to the full Senate. The Senate did not address the treaty before the November elections. The Administration pressed the Senate to debate the treaty during the lame-

---

[35] U.S. Congress, Senate Committee on Foreign Relations, *Treaty with Russia on Measures for Further Reduction and Limitation of Strategic Offensive Arms (The New START Treaty)*, Executive Report , 111th Cong., 2nd sess., October 1, 2010, Exec. Rept 111-6 (Washington: GPO, 2010).

[36] Josh Rogin, "Kerry and DeMint Spar over Missile Defense," *Foreign Policy, The Cable*, September 16, 2010. http://thecable.foreignpolicy.com/posts/2010/09/16/kerry_and_demint_spar_over_missile_defense See, also, John Isaacs, Analysis of the Senate Foreign Relations Committee Passage of the new START Treaty, *The Chain Reaction*, September, 16, 2010. http://blog.livableworld.org/story/2010/9/16/16585/7341

---

duck session of Congress in December 2010. Many Senators supported this goal. Some, however, suggested that the Senate would not have time to debate the treaty during the lame-duck session, and indicated that they preferred the Senate wait until 2011 to debate the treaty.

The Senate began the debate on New START on December 16, 2010. During the debate, some Senators proposed amendments to the treaty, both to strike language related to ballistic missile defenses and to add language related to nonstrategic nuclear weapons. The treaty's supporters argued that these amendments would "kill" the treaty because they would require Russian approval and could lead to the reopening of negotiations on a wide range of issues addressed in the treaty. The Senate rejected these amendments, but it did accept amendments to the Resolution of Ratification that underlined the U.S. commitment to modernizing its nuclear weapons infrastructure and its commitment to deploying ballistic missile defenses. In addition, President Obama sent a letter to the Senators confirming his view that the New START Treaty places "no limitations on the development or deployment of our missile defense programs," highlighting his commitment to proceed with the deployment of all four phases of the missile defense system planned for Europe, and noting that the continued development and deployment of U.S. missile defenses would not threaten the strategic balance with Russia and would not "constitute the basis for questioning the effectiveness and viability of the New START Treaty."[37]

The Senate gave its advice and consent to ratification of New START on December 22, 2010, approving the Resolution of Ratification by a vote of 71-26. President Obama signed the instruments of ratification in early February 2011.

Russian Ratification Process

Russia's President Medvedev submitted the New START Treaty to the Russian Parliament on May 28, 2010. Both Houses of the Russian Parliament, the Duma and the Federation Council, will vote on the treaty, with a majority vote required to approve the law on ratification. Russia's president said he hoped that the two sides could "synchronize" their ratification, voting on the treaty at about the same time. This would avoid the circumstances that existed on the second START Treaty in the late 1990s, when the U.S. Senate gave its consent to ratification of START II in January 1996, but by the time the Russian Parliament voted in 2000, the parties had negotiated a Protocol to the Treaty that also required ratification. The Senate never voted on the new version of the treaty, and START II never entered into force. Most experts agree that President Medvedev should be able to win approval for the treaty in the Russian Parliament with little difficulty.

The Foreign Affairs Committee of the Russian Duma had initially supported the treaty. However, in early November 2010, Konstantin Kosachev, the head of the committee, indicated that the committee would reconsider the treaty. He indicated that this was in response to both the delay in the U.S. Senate's consideration of the treaty and the conditions and understandings that the Senate Foreign Relations Committee included in the U.S. Resolution of Ratification. Nevertheless, after the Senate voted on the treaty on December 22, members of the Duma called for the prompt ratification of New START. Reports indicated they received the documents from the Senate on December 23, and they held their first vote on the Draft Law on Ratification by Friday, December 24. The Duma then crafted amendments and declarations to the Federal Law on Ratification, and,

---

[37] http://www.america.gov/st/texttrans-english/2010/December/20101220112111su0.6327565 html.

after two more votes, approved the treaty by a vote of 350-96 (with one abstention) on January 25, 2011.

The upper chamber of Russia's parliament, the Federation Council, also voted on the ratification of the treaty. Sergei Mironov, the Speaker of the Federation Council, indicated that the vote would take place after the vote in the Duma.[38] This occurred on January 26, 2011, when the Federation Council unanimously approved the ratification of the treaty.[39] President Medvedev signed the instruments of ratification on January 28, 2011. Russia's Federal Law on Ratification contains a number of declarations and understandings that highlight the Duma and Federation Council's concerns with the New START Treaty. These do not alter the text of the treaty and, therefore, will not require U.S. consent or agreement. Many of the provisions in the law call on Russia's leadership to pursue funding for the modernization and sustainment of Russia's strategic nuclear forces. They also reiterate Russia's view that that the preamble to the treaty, and its reference to the relationship between offensive and defense forces, is an integral part of the treaty. The law does not indicate that this language imposes any restrictions on the United States. It does, however, reiterate that that Russia has a right to withdraw from the treaty, and could do so if the United States deploys defenses that undermine Russia's strategic deterrent. In addition, the law indicates that new kinds of strategic offensive weapons, such as the potential U.S. conventional prompt global strike weapons, should count under the treaty limits. The law indicates that the parties should meet in the BCC and agree on how to count these systems before either party deploys the system. This differs from the U.S. interpretation because the United States has indicated that it could deploy such systems before completing the discussions in the BCC. These differing interpretations should not delay the entry into force of the treaty, but could raise questions in the future, if the United States deploys a PGS system that it does not consider to count under the treaty limits.

Entry into Force and Implementation

Secretary Clinton and Foreign Minister Lavrov exchanged the instruments of ratification for the New START Treaty on February 5, 2011. This act brought the treaty into force and started the clock on early activities outlined in the treaty. For example, the United States and Russia conducted their initial data exchange, 45 days after the treaty entered into force, on March 22, 2011, within 45 days of entry into force. They also had the right to begin on-site inspection activities in early April, 60 days after the treaty entered into force. Reports indicate that this process began in the United States with the display of a B-1 bomber and in Russia with the display of Russia's new RS-24 missile.

The United States and Russia also met in Geneva, from March 28 through April 8, 2011, in the first meeting of the treaty's Bilateral Consultative Commission. The representatives issued two joint statements at the conclusion of the meeting that addressed procedures that would be used during the on-site inspection process. The parties met for the second session of the BCC from October 19 to November 2, 2011.

The third meeting of the BCC occurred in late January 2012. During that meeting, the parties signed several statements on the sharing telemetry on missile test launches. They agreed that they

---

[38] "Federation Council Ready to Ratify New START on Same Day as Duma - Mironov," *Interfax*, December 23, 2010.

[39] "Russian Parliament Approves START Nuclear Arms Treaty," *BBC News*, January 26, 2011.

would exchange telemetric data on one ICBM or SLBM launch that had occurred between February 5, 2011, when the treaty entered into force, and the end of 2011. They also agreed on when they would begin and end the sharing of telemetric data during the flight test of an ICBM or SLBM. They also agreed on the procedures they would use when demonstrating the recording media and playback equipment used when providing telemetric information.[40]

In a data exchange released in February 2011, with numbers drawn from the treaty's initial data exchange, the U.S. State Department noted that the United States had 1,800 warheads on 882 deployed ICBMs, deployed SLBMs, and deployed heavy bombers.[41] These deployed forces were within a total of 1,124 deployed and nondeployed launchers of ICBMs and SLBMs, and deployed in nondeployed heavy bombers. By September 2011, the United States had reduced these numbers to 1,790 warheads on 882 deployed ICBMs, deployed SLBMs, and deployed heavy bombers.[42] The total number of deployed and nondeployed launchers had declined to 1,043. The State Department did not provide details of how the United States had altered its forces, but, with the number of deployed launchers remaining the same, it is likely that the United States withdrew 10 warheads from deployed ICBMs or SLBMs. The reduction in 81 nondeployed launchers likely reflects the conversion or elimination of some of the "phantom" launchers that remained in the U.S. force but no longer carried nuclear warheads.

The State Department releases also include the summary of Russia's force data. In February 2011, Russia reported that it had 1,537 warheads on 521 deployed ICBMs, deployed SLBMs, and deployed heavy bombers. Russia also reported a total of 865 deployed and nondeployed delivery vehicles. At the time of this report, analysts expressed surprise that Russian forces were already below the treaty limits in New START when the treaty entered into force. Some argued that this indicated the United States did not have to sign the treaty to bring about reductions in Russian forces, and that the treaty represented unilateral concessions by the United States. Others noted that the number of deployed warheads possibly reflected the ongoing retirement of older Russian missiles and could change in the future as Russia deployed new, multiple-warhead land-based missiles. In September 2011, in the second treaty data exchange, Russia reported that it had 1,566 deployed warheads on 516 deployed ICBMs, deployed SLBMs, and deployed heavy bombers. Hence, although the number of deployed delivery vehicles declined, the number of warheads increased by a small amount, and now exceeds the treaty limit of 1,550 warheads. Because the data provides no details of the force composition, this increase could either be due to the deployment of the new MIRVed RS-24 missiles, which carry more warheads than the single-warhead SS-25 missile they replace, or due to variations in the numbers of warheads carried on deployed SLBMs. The number of deployed and nondeployed delivery vehicles had also increased slightly, to 871. This could reflect the retirement of some of Russia's older missiles, which would move their delivery vehicles from the deployed to nondeployed column in the data.

In a joint briefing provided by the United States and Russia in October 2011, the parties also reported on their progress in implementing the monitoring regime in New START. They noted that, in the first six months of treaty implementation, they had exchanged almost 1,500 notifications and had conducted demonstrations of telemetric information playback equipment.

---

[40] For the text of these three statements, see, U.S. Department of State, Bureau of Arms Control, Verification, and Compliance, http://www.state.gov/t/avc/rls/183540 htm, http://www.state.gov/t/avc/rls/183541.htm, http://www.state.gov/t/avc/rls/183539 htm.

[41] http://www.state.gov/t/avc/rls/164722 htm.

[42] http://www.state.gov/t/avc/rls/175945 htm.

By end of the first year of implementation, on February 5, 2012, the parties had exchanged over 1,800 notifications. They had also conducted three required exhibitions, with Russia exhibiting the RS-24 missile and its launcher, and the United States exhibiting the B-1 and B-2 bombers. During the year, both parties had also conducted all 18 of the permitted inspections at facilities in the other nation. These inspections occurred at ICBM, SLBM, and heavy bomber bases; storage facilities; conversion and elimination facilities; and test ranges.[43]

Issues for Congress

New START and Strategic Stability

When the Obama Administration released the 2010 Nuclear Posture Review, it indicated that the United States would retain a triad of ICBMs, SLBMs, and heavy bombers under the New START Treaty. The NPR indicates that this force structure supports strategic stability because it allows the United States to maintain an "assured second-strike capability" with warheads on survivable ballistic missile submarines and allows the United States to retain "sufficient force structure in each leg to ... hedge effectively ... if necessary due to unexpected technological problems or operational vulnerabilities."[44]

Administration officials have also indicated that New START promotes strategic stability by "discounting" the weapons on heavy bombers. As President Reagan argued during his commencement address at Eureka College in 1982, ballistic missiles are the "most destabilizing nuclear systems."[45] As a result, in his START proposals, President Reagan sought deep reductions in ballistic missile warheads, but lesser reductions in the weapons on heavy bombers. The counting rules in New START reflect this logic. Because bomber weapons would take hours or days to reach their targets, and because they could be recalled after they were launched, they pose less of a threat to strategic stability than do ballistic missiles. As a result, some argue that, even if the United States and Russia retain hundreds of bomber weapons that do not count against the treaty limits, the reductions required in ballistic missile warheads will enhance strategic stability.

Some have also noted that New START may strengthen strategic stability from the Russian perspective by removing the specific limits and restrictions on mobile ICBMs. Russia does not deploy many submarines at sea, and, therefore, lacks an assured second-strike capability on that leg of its triad. Instead, it has sought to improve the survivability of its forces by deploying ICBMs on mobile launchers. Under START, the United States sought to restrict these systems because it feared it would not be able to count them in peacetime and target them in wartime. In the current environment, concerns about wartime targeting played less of a role in the negotiations. Consequently, instead of limiting their numbers and restricting their operations, New START seeks to provide transparency and openness, so the United States can be confident in

---

[43] U.S. Department of State, Bureau of Arms Control, Verification, and Compliance, *New START Treaty Implementation Update*, Washington, D.C., February 5, 2012, http://www.state.gov/t/avc/rls/183335 htm.

[44] U.S. Department of Defense, *Nuclear Posture Review*, Washington, DC, April 6, 2010, p. 20, http://www.defense.gov/npr/docs/2010%20Nuclear%20Posture%20Review%20Report.pdf.

[45] Ronald Reagan, Commencement Address at Eureka College, May 9, 1982. http://www.presidency.ucsb.edu/ws/index.php?pid=42501.

its ability to count these weapons in peacetime even though it might not be able to attack them during a conflict.

Critics of the New START Treaty have questioned whether it serves U.S. security interests even if it does promote strategic stability. Some argued, during the negotiations, that the United States did not need to negotiate a new treaty to maintain its own triad, as this was possible with or without arms control. They also argued that the United States did not need to reduce its forces to bring about reductions in Russia's forces, as Russia would reduce its forces over the next decade as it retired aging systems, even in the absence of a new arms control agreement.[46] Moreover, they question whether arms control should even be a part of the U.S.-Russian relationship as arms control is a symbol of a Cold War, antagonistic relationship between the two nations. They believe that the United States and Russia should not measure their relationship with each other using Cold War-era measures like strategic stability and survivable warheads.

Some of these same critics, however, have argued that New START is flawed because it will not limit the number of nondeployed missiles for mobile ICBM launchers. They argue that, during a conflict, Russia could reload these launchers with stored warheads, or mate them with nondeployed launchers, and vastly increase its ability to strike targets in the United States. As a result, they argue, the treaty would not strengthen stability and could undermine the security of the United States.

While it is true that New START does not limit nondeployed ICBMs, many in the United States no longer consider missiles in storage to be a threat to U.S. security. The treaty allows the United States to keep track of the numbers and locations of stored missiles. Moreover, these numbers are not likely to grow quickly during the life of the treaty because Russia produces so few missiles each year that it would find it difficult to maintain the size of its deployed force and augment its nondeployed stockpile. Moreover, it seems inconsistent to criticize the treaty negotiations on the grounds that they perpetuate a Cold War relationship that no longer exists, then to criticize the treaty on the grounds that it does not address a concern with mobile ICBMs that derives from that Cold War-era relationship.

Monitoring and Verification in New START

Monitoring and verification have been among the central concerns addressed in the Senate committees during their review of the New START Treaty. The cooperative monitoring measures in the treaty may receive special scrutiny, as many observers of the arms control process specifically measured the value of the monitoring and verification regime in the original START Treaty by its widespread use of notifications, on-site inspections, and other cooperative measures.

Some critics of New START have questioned whether the monitoring provisions in the new treaty are sufficient to provide the United States with enough information to either confirm Russian compliance with the treaty or to detect efforts to violate its terms. They point to differences between the verification regime in the original START Treaty and those in New START to argue that the new verification regime is less robust than the old regime. They note that the United States will no longer maintain a monitoring presence outside the Votkinsk facility where Russia assembles its mobile ICBMs, which may weaken the U.S. ability to count these missiles as they

---

[46] Keith B. Payne, "Evaluating the U.S.-Russia Nuclear Deal," *Wall Street Journal*, April 8, 2010, p. A21.

enter Russia's forces. They also note that the United States and Russia will no longer exchange telemetry data on all their ballistic missile flight tests, which, over time, could lessen the U.S. ability to understand and evaluate the capabilities of Russian ballistic missiles.

The Obama Administration and others who support the new treaty have argued that the verification regime in New START will be more than sufficient to provide the United States with confidence in Russia's compliance with the treaty. They acknowledge that the regime is different from the regime in the original START Treaty, but note that this is, in part, due to improvements in the relationship between Russia and the United States and differences between the limits and restrictions in the two treaties. They argue that the monitoring regime in New START is streamlined, both to reduce its costs and to ease the disruptions caused by monitoring for U.S. and Russian military forces. They also note that it relies on as much or more cooperation between the two parties, which will continue to build confidence and reduce suspicions.

Moreover, many in the Administration have noted that the United States has not had any opportunity to monitor Russian forces on Russian territory since the original treaty expired in December 2009. They argued that continuing delays in Senate consideration of New START could further reduce U.S. and Russian confidence in their knowledge of each others forces, leading to worst-case assessments and possible instabilities. They further remind those who contend that the verification regime in New START is less robust than the regime in old START, that the absence of a treaty means the absence of any monitoring and verification regime. The United States does not have the option of returning the regime of the original START Treaty; nor should it want to do so since the new treaty has different limits and restrictions than the old treaty. Many U.S. officials, including Admiral Mullen and General Chilton, have included their concerns about the absence of monitoring in their appeals for the prompt ratification of the New START Treaty.

Questions about the monitoring and verification regime in New START go beyond concerns about the specific monitoring mechanisms and the U.S. ability to confirm Russian compliance with individual limits in the treaty. Most experts agree that neither party can be absolutely certain that the other is in perfect compliance with all the limits and restrictions in the treaty. This is due, in some cases, to ambiguities in the treaty language and varying interpretations of the treaty requirements. It is also due to the fact that both sides may have gaps in their knowledge about the details of the other side's forces and activities. These uncertainties do not, by themselves, indicate that the parties should not ratify and implement the treaty. The broader question often asked by experts on treaty monitoring and verification is whether the parties, in general, and the United States, in particular, will have high confidence in Russia's compliance with the treaty, and, in those cases when compliance concerns may come up, whether the United States will be able to detect evidence of potential violations that might undermine U.S. security with enough warning to respond and adjust U.S. forces to offset those security concerns.

The Obama Administration has indicated, in documents submitted to the Senate in July 2010, that the New START Treaty meets this standard. The Administration concluded that the benefits to Russia of cheating would be minimal, as the United States, by maintaining a triad of ICBMs, SLBMs, and bombers, would be able to respond to any attempt to shift the strategic balance by adding significant numbers of warheads to its own forces. Moreover, if Russia were to cheat to any significant degree, it would undermine its relationship with the United States and interfere with any possible future arms control agreements. Therefore, in a letter sent to the Senate Foreign

Relations Committee in September 2010, Secretary of Defense Gates concluded that Russia would not be able to achieve "militarily significant cheating" under the New START Treaty.[47]

A review of the verification regime in New START, and summary of some of the differences between the verification regime in the original START Treaty and the regime in New START can be found in CRS Report R41201, *Monitoring and Verification in Arms Control*.

New START and Ballistic Missile Defenses

As was noted above, the Administration has testified repeatedly that the New START Treaty imposes no limits on current or planned ballistic missile defense programs in the United States. Some critics have claimed, however, that the United States might impose those limits itself, to ensure that Russia does not withdraw from New START, as it said it might do in the unilateral statement it released when it signed the treaty.

Officials from the Obama Administration have argued that this concern is unfounded. They have noted that the Soviet Union issued a similar statement when it signed the original START Treaty, threatening to withdraw if the United States withdrew from the 1972 Anti-ballistic Missile (ABM Treaty). Yet, when the United States withdrew from the ABM Treaty in 2002, Russia not only did not withdraw from START, it continued to participate in negotiations on the 2002 Strategic Offensive Reductions Treaty. Moreover, in the 1990s, when the United States might have altered its missile defense plans in response to the Soviet letter, the United States actually expanded its missile defense activities and increased spending on missile defense programs. As a result, there is little reason, based on historical data, to expect the United States to restrain its missile defense programs. Moreover, officials from the Obama Administration have highlighted that the Ballistic Missile Defense Review, the Nuclear Posture Review, and the 2011 budget all offer strong support for continuing U.S. missile defense programs.[48]

Some critics have also claimed that Russia might seek, and the United States might agree to, new limits on U.S. missile defense capabilities in the Bilateral Consultative Commission established by the treaty. According to the Protocol to New START, this commission is designed "to promote the implementation of the provisions of the Treaty." The Protocol indicates that the United States and Russia will meet in the commission to "resolve questions relating to compliance with the obligations assumed by the Parties," agree on "additional measures as may be necessary to improve the viability and effectiveness of the Treaty," and "discuss other issues raised by either Party." Some have claimed that because this agenda is somewhat open-ended, Russia may raise its concerns about U.S. missile defenses in the commission and propose limits on those systems.

The Obama Administration has insisted that the parties could not, and would not use the BCC to negotiate new limits on ballistic missile defenses or any other elements of the U.S. strategic arsenal. In a fact sheet that accompanies the treaty, the State Department has indicated that the parties would use the BCC "to reach agreement on changes in the Protocol to the Treaty, including its Annexes, that do not affect substantive rights or obligations. The BCC may in no way make changes that would affect the substantive rights and obligations contained in the New

---

[47] Robert Burns, "Gates: Any Russian Arms Cheating Would Backfire," *Associated Press*, September 9, 2010.

[48] U.S. State Department, Bureau of Verification, Compliance, and Implementation, *Ballistic Missile Defense and the New START Treaty*, Fact Sheet, Washington, DC, April 21, 2010, http://www.state.gov/t/vci/rls/140624 htm.

START Treaty."[49] The parties may use the BCC to "agree upon such additional measures as may be necessary to improve the viability and effectiveness of the Treaty" but these measures would address concerns that came up while implementing the existing limits and restrictions in the treaty. They would not be able to impose new limits or restrictions without amending the treaty, and any amendment to the treaty would be subject to the same ratification process as the treaty itself. The Senate would have to offer its advice and consent.

Modernization

The New START Treaty does not limit or restrict the ability of the United States or Russia to modernize strategic offensive nuclear forces. It specifically states, in Article V, paragraph 1, that, "Subject to the provisions of this Treaty, modernization and replacement of strategic offensive arms may be carried out."

Although the treaty does not restrict weapons modernization, some Members of Congress and analysts outside government have questioned whether the United States is sufficiently committed to modernizing and maintaining its strategic nuclear forces, nuclear weapons complex, and nuclear warheads. The FY2010 Defense Authorization Act includes a provision (P.L. 111-84, §1251) that required the Administration to submit a report to Congress when it submitted the New START Treaty to the Senate that described how it planned to "enhance the safety, security, and reliability of the nuclear weapons stockpile of the United States; modernize the nuclear weapons complex; and maintain the delivery platforms for nuclear weapons." In this 1251 report, the Administration stated that the United States planned to spend $180 billion over the next 10 years to meet these objectives, with $80 billion allocated to the U.S. nuclear weapons complex and nuclear warheads and $100 billion allocated to the Navy and Air Force for the maintenance and modernization of their delivery systems. These totals did not include any modernization programs that were planned to occur after the 10-year time frame.

Some Members of Congress and analysts outside the government have questioned whether the funding in this program would be sufficient to maintain and sustain the U.S. nuclear arsenal. Some argued that the totals did not add enough above the previously planned program to go far in expanding the U.S. capability to maintain and modernize its forces. Others questioned whether the Administration would sustain its commitment for more than a year or two, particularly in an era of tight defense budgets.

Others, however, have argued that the Administration's budget for the nuclear weapons complex in FY2011 and the added funding outlined in the 1251 report demonstrate a strong commitment to recapitalizing the U.S. nuclear weapons complex, maintaining nuclear warheads, and maintaining and modernizing the delivery vehicles. The Administration added nearly 10%, or over $700 million, to the DOE budget for nuclear weapons in FY2011. Ambassador Linton Brooks, who had served as the Director of the National Nuclear Security Administration during the Bush Administration, indicated that he would have "killed" for a budget of that magnitude when he was managing the nuclear weapons complex for DOE.[50] While there are no assurances that Congress will approve these increases and continue to fund the weapons programs at this level for the

---

[49] http://www.state.gov/t/vci/rls/145830 htm.

[50] http://csis.org/blog/ambassador-linton-brooks-new-start-and-next-treaty.

duration of the New START Treaty, the Administration has argued that there should be little doubt about its commitment to modernize the complex and maintain U.S. nuclear weapons capabilities.

Nonstrategic Nuclear Weapons

Presidents Obama and Medvedev agreed, in April 2009, when they initiated the negotiations on the New START Treaty, that this agreement would address only strategic nuclear forces, the long-range weapons that each side could use to reach the territory of the other side. It would not seek to limit or restrict the shorter-range nonstrategic nuclear weapons in either side's arsenal. This agreement derived not only from the fact that the existing START Treaty, and nearly all past bilateral arms control treaties, had addressed only strategic nuclear weapons, but also from the fact that many of the issues that would need to be addressed in a treaty that limited nonstrategic nuclear weapons would likely prove too complex to resolve in the near term, when both sides sought to replace the existing START Treaty.

There is widespread agreement in Congress, in the Obama Administration, and within the arms control community, that the United States and Russia should seek to negotiate a treaty that increases transparency and possibly imposes limits on nonstrategic strategic nuclear weapons.[51] However, there is also widespread agreement that negotiating such a treaty would prove extremely difficult, as Russia maintains a far larger stock of these weapons than the United States, in part to compensate for perceived weaknesses in its conventional forces, and because U.S. nonstrategic nuclear weapons are a part of the U.S. commitment to NATO, and the United States believes that any changes in their deployment should be addressed by the alliance before they are addressed in an arms control negotiation.

Some analysts and Senators have questioned whether the United States should agree to limit its strategic nuclear weapons in the absence of any limits on Russian nonstrategic nuclear weapons. They note that Russia retains approximately 3,800 nonstrategic nuclear weapons while the United States has fewer than 400 in Europe, and that the value of these weapons could grow as the numbers of U.S. and Russian strategic nuclear weapons decline. They also note that these weapons could seem particularly threatening to some of the new NATO states that are located near the periphery of Russia. Others however, argue that Russian nonstrategic nuclear weapons do not pose a threat to the United States or NATO, as Russia has indicated that these weapons would only be used in response to an attack on Russian territory. So, these analysts note, as long as NATO does not initiate such an attack, NATO members would not be threatened by these weapons. Moreover, as Senator Lugar noted in his response to former Massachusetts Governor Mitt Romney's critique of New START, most of Russia's nonstrategic nuclear weapons do not pose a missile threat to Europe. Senator Lugar stated that "most of Russia's tactical nuclear weapons either have very short ranges, are used for homeland air defense, are devoted to the Chinese border, or are in storage."[52]

Many of the experts who testified in support of the New START Treaty agreed that the United States and Russia should pursue negotiations on a treaty on nonstrategic nuclear weapons. However, most agreed that Russia would be unwilling to participate in such discussions, and the

---

[51] For a description of U.S. and Russian nonstrategic nuclear weapons see CRS Report RL32572, *Nonstrategic Nuclear Weapons*, by Amy F. Woolf.

[52] Press Release of Senator Richard Lugar. "Lugar: Romney Misinformed on New START Treaty." July 8, 2010. http://lugar.senate.gov/news/record.cfm?id=326277&&

United States and Russia would be unlikely to find common ground on such an agreement, unless both sides ratified and implemented the New START Treaty first. For example, in testimony before the Senate Foreign Relations Committee on April 29, 2010, former Secretaries of Defense James Schlesinger and William Perry both indicated that nonstrategic nuclear weapons should be an issue for the next treaty, and that the United States should ratify New START as a step on the path to get to reduction in nonstrategic nuclear weapons.[53]

New START and the U.S. Nuclear Nonproliferation Agenda

The Obama Administration has argued that U.S.-Russian cooperation on arms control, in general, and the New START Treaty, specifically, can help move forward the U.S. and international nuclear nonproliferation agenda. No one has argued that the treaty will convince nations who are seeking their own nuclear weapon that they should follow the U.S. and Russian lead and reduce those weapons or roll back those programs. However, some have argued that U.S.-Russian cooperation on arms control could strengthen the U.S.-Russian cooperation on a broader array of issues and that, "cooperation is a prerequisite for moving forward with tough, internationally binding sanctions on Iran."[54]

Moreover, some have noted that U.S.-Russian cooperation on arms control will also demonstrate that these nations are living up to their obligations under the Nuclear Nonproliferation Treaty (NPT).[55] Most nations that are parties to the NPT believe that reductions in the number of deployed nuclear weapons are a clear indicator of U.S. and Russian compliance with their obligations under Article VI of the NPT.[56] During the preparatory committee meetings (PrepComs) leading up to the 2010 Review Conference of the NPT, many of the participants called on the United States and Russia to complete negotiations on a New START Treaty. While the completion of this treaty may not assure the United States of widespread agreement on U.S. goals and priorities at the NPT review conference, many argue that the absence of an agreement would have certainly complicated U.S. efforts and reduced the chances for a successful conference.

In contrast, some have argued that the New START Treaty will do little to advance U.S. nonproliferation goals. They argue that the parties at the NPT review conference may express their approval of the new treaty, but their positions on substantive issues will reflect their own national security interests and goals. Moreover, some critics argue that the new treaty has been a distraction and the United States would have used its time better working directly to implement crippling sanctions on Iran. Finally, some argue that the New START Treaty, and the NPR, may undermine U.S. nonproliferation goals by calling into question U.S. security commitments and the continuing salience of U.S. nuclear weapons.

---

[53] U.S. Congress, Senate Committee on Foreign Relations, *Senate Foreign Relations Committee Holds Hearing on U.S.-Russia Arms Control Cooperation*, Hearing, 111th Cong., 2nd sess., April 29, 2010.

[54] Under Secretary of State Ellen Tauscher, *The Case for New START Ratification*, Atlantic Council Panel Discussion, April 21, 2010. http://www.state.gov/t/us/140633 htm.

[55] Ibid.

[56] Article VI states that the parties to the treaty will "pursue negotiations in good faith on effective measures relating to cessation of the nuclear arms race at an early date and to nuclear disarmament, and on a Treaty on general and complete disarmament under strict and effective international control." http://www.state.gov/t/isn/trty/16281 htm.

Arms Control after New START

The Obama Administration indicated that the New START Treaty would be the first step in a renewed arms control process with Russia. In his statement on April 8, 2010, when the United States and Russia signed the treaty, President Obama indicated that "this treaty will set the stage for further cuts. And going forward, we hope to pursue discussions with Russia on reducing both our strategic and tactical weapons, including nondeployed weapons."[57]

Many analysts hoped the New START Treaty would cut more deeply into U.S. and Russian forces, reducing them to perhaps 1,000 warheads on each side. Others objected to the START format because the Presidents agreed the new treaty would not contain limits on nonstrategic nuclear weapons or nondeployed nuclear warheads. A second treaty would likely address some of these concerns. But a new treaty that addressed each of these issues could be extremely difficult to complete. Russia may not be willing to negotiate reductions in its nonstrategic nuclear weapons, and neither side may be willing to adopt the amount of transparency necessary to negotiate verifiable limits on nondeployed warheads in storage. Moreover, before the number of deployed warheads can decline much further, Russia may again insist on negotiating limits on U.S. missile defense programs. And some speculate that, if the United States and Russia reduce their forces below 1,000 deployed warheads, the negotiations would have to include China, France, and Great Britain, the other declared nuclear weapons states under the NPT.

Moreover, some analysts and Members of Congress do not believe that new START should be the first of many steps on a renewed arms control agenda because they object to many of the potential additional steps on this agenda. They would not support a treaty that imposed deeper reductions on U.S. strategic nuclear weapons or one that imposed limits on nondeployed nuclear weapons. They would object to the ratification and implementation of the Comprehensive Test Ban Treaty, which may be next on the Obama Administration's arms control agenda, and they object strongly to the President's vision of a world free of nuclear weapons, which he endorsed in his speech in Prague on April 5, 2009. Hence, some who have concluded that the New START Treaty would not harm U.S. security by itself, have objected to its ratification because they believe its defeat will close the door on the rest of the President's arms control agenda.

Author Contact Information

Amy F. Woolf
Specialist in Nuclear Weapons Policy
awoolf@crs.loc.gov, 7-2379

---

[57] "Remarks by President Obama and President Medvedev of Russia at New START Signing Ceremony and Press Conference." April 8, 2010. Available at http://www.whitehouse.gov/the-press-office/remarks-president-obama-and-president-medvedev-russia-new-start-treaty-signing-cere.